낭독하는 명작동화

Level 3-3

Mulan

✦ 뮬란 ✦

새벽달(남수진) • 이현석 지음

How to Use

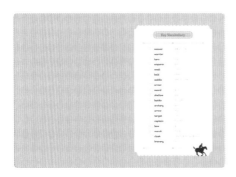

Key Vocabulary

명작동화를 읽기 전에 스토리의 **핵심 단어**를 확인해 보세요. 내가 알고 있는 단어라면 체크 표시하고, 모르는 단어는 이야기를 읽은 후에 체크 표시해 보세요.

Story

Level 3의 영어 텍스트 수준은 책의 난이도를 측정하는 레벨 지수인 **AR(Accelerated Reader) 지수 2.5~3.3 사이**로 미국 **초등학생 2~3학년 수준**으로 맞추고, 분량을 **1100 단어 내외**로 구성했습니다.

쉬운 단어와 간결한 문장으로 구성된 스토리를 그림과 함께 읽어 보세요 페이지마다 내용 이해를 돕는 그림이 있어 상상력을 풍부하게 해 주며, 이야기를 더욱 재미있게 읽을 수 있습니다.

Reading Training

이현석 선생님의 **강세와 청킹 가이드**에 맞춰 명작동화를 낭독해 보세요.

한국어 번역으로 내용을 확인하고 **우리말 낭독**을 하는 것도 좋습니다.

This Book

Storytelling

명작동화의 내용을 떠올릴 수 있는 **8개의 그림**이 준비되어 있습니다. 각 그림당 제시된 **3개의 단어**를 활용하여 이야기를 만들고 말해 보세요. 상상력과 창의력을 기르는 데 큰 도움이 될 것입니다.

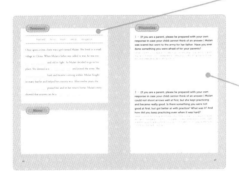

Summary

명작동화의 **줄거리 요약문**이 제시되어 있습니다. 빈칸에 들어갈 단어를 채워 보며 이야기의 내용을 다시 정리해 보세요.

Discussion

명작동화의 내용을 실생활에 응용하거나 비판적으로 생각해 볼 수 있는 **토론 질문**으로 구성했습니다. 영어 또는 우리말로 토론하며 책의 내용을 재구성해 보세요.

픽처 텔링 카드

특별부록으로 **16장의 이야기 그림 카드**가 맨 뒷장에 있어 한 장씩 뜯어서 활용이 가능합니다. 순서에 맞게 그림을 배열하고 이야기 말하기를 해 보세요.

QR코드 영상을 통해 새벽달님과 이현석 선생님이 이 책을 활용하는 가장 좋은 방법을 직접 설명해 드립니다!

Contents

Mulan

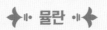

◆▮• 뮬란 •▮◆

Key Vocabulary

- [ ] **weaver** — 베를 짜는 사람
- [ ] **warrior** — 전사
- [ ] **hero** — 영웅
- [ ] **emperor** — 황제
- [ ] **weak** — 쇠약한
- [ ] **bold** — 대담한
- [ ] **saddle** — (말에 얹는) 안장
- [ ] **armor** — 갑옷
- [ ] **sword** — 칼, 검
- [ ] **shallow** — 얕은
- [ ] **battle** — 전쟁, 전투
- [ ] **archery** — 활쏘기
- [ ] **arrow** — 화살
- [ ] **target** — 과녁
- [ ] **captain** — 장군, 지도자
- [ ] **bow** — 활
- [ ] **march** — 행군하다
- [ ] **clash** — (부딪쳐) 쨍 하는 소리를 내다
- [ ] **bravery** — 용기

Once there was a girl named Mulan.
She lived in a small village in China.
She had a kind father and a loving mother.
She also had a playful younger brother.

Mulan loved to play outside.
She could climb trees and run fast.
She laughed a lot every day.
Her laugh made her family smile.

Mulan's father and mother were weavers.

They made beautiful clothes.

Sometimes, Mulan's father told her great stories.

They were about warriors and heroes.

Mulan liked to hear those stories.

She did not want to be a weaver.

She wanted to be a hero someday.

She dreamed of adventures.

One day, Mulan's family got a letter.

It was from the emperor.

The emperor needed soldiers to fight for the country.

The soldiers had to go to Black Mountain.

The name of Mulan's father was on the list.

Mulan's father was once a great soldier.

But now, he was a weak old man.

Mulan saw her father's worried face.

"I am weak. But I will fight for my country," said her father.

But Mulan felt a big sadness in her heart.

'If father goes, he may die.

My brother is too young to go,' she thought.

She could not let her father go.

That night, Mulan had an idea.

It was a big and bold idea.

She was going to be a soldier.

'I will do it for my father!' she thought.

The next day, Mulan woke up early.

She acted on her idea.

Mulan went to the market in the East.

And she bought a big and strong horse.

Mulan also went to the market in the West.

And she bought a saddle.

Mulan then went to the market in the North.

And she bought a big and heavy armor.

Finally, Mulan went to the market in the South.

She bought a sharp sword.

Night came, and Mulan tied her hair up.
She looked like a man.
'I am all ready,' Mulan thought.

Mulan did not want to wake her family.
She said goodbye to them in her heart.

Mulan got onto her horse.
She rode into the night.
It was dark, so she felt scared.
But she wanted to be brave.
She was going to be a hero.

Mulan rode for many hours.
She went over mountains and crossed shallow rivers.
The horse was very fast.
It looked like it was flying.

The stars shone brightly above Mulan.
The moon led her way.
Mulan thought about her family.
She missed them already.
But she knew she was doing the right thing.

Mulan stopped at the Yellow River.

She slept there with her horse.

In the morning, Mulan arrived at Black Mountain.

She saw many soldiers.

'They look very strong,' Mulan thought.

She took a deep breath.

She was ready to start her big adventure.

Mulan trained well with the other soldiers.

She was strong, and she became stronger.

No one knew she was a woman.

Mulan also learned to ride a horse in a battle.

She loved riding her strong and fast horse.

When she rode her horse, she felt free.

Mulan also learned archery.
At first, the arrows missed the target.
But she kept trying.
Soon, she was able to hit the target.
Other young soldiers clapped for her.

Mulan soon made friends in the camp.
They liked her because she was strong and kind.
The captain always wanted Mulan by his side.
He knew she was a great soldier.

At night, Mulan thought about her home.
She looked at the stars and felt a little sad.
She missed her mother, father, and brother.
But she knew she was doing something important.

Days turned into weeks.
Mulan became a brave and strong soldier.
She was ready to fight in battles.

Then one day, the captain had big news.
There was going to be a battle.
The soldiers had to fight the enemy.
Mulan felt a little scared but also ready.
She remembered her training.

The soldiers put on their armors and got ready.
They took their swords and bows.
The captain told the soldiers to be strong and brave.
Mulan listened and nodded.
She remembered her family and felt braver.

The soldiers marched to the battlefield.
Mulan saw the enemy but she was not afraid.
She was ready to fight for her country.

The battle began with loud noises.
The soldiers ran as fast as they could.
Swords clashed, and arrows were shot.
Mulan fought with all her heart.

Mulan used her sword and her bow.
She was fast, strong, and smart.
She helped her captain many times.
Her captain also helped her many times.

Then Mulan saw the captain of the enemy.
He was trying to hurt her friends.
He moved fast, but Mulan moved faster.
She used her bow and got rid of him.

The enemy saw Mulan's bravery and strength.
They were scared and ran away.
Mulan helped her country win the battle.
Everyone cheered and clapped.
They were happy and proud.

After the battle, the captain thanked Mulan.

"You are the bravest soldier," he said.

"You are my good friend, too."

Mulan smiled, feeling very proud.

Mulan became famous among all the soldiers.

The captain took her to all the battles.

Mulan fought many battles and won.

She was a soldier for twelve years.

She was tired but happy.

The captain told the emperor about Mulan.
"He is a good soldier!
I want to see him," said the emperor.
Then, he invited Mulan to the palace.

"I heard you are a good soldier.
Ask me anything you wish to have," said the emperor.
Mulan did not need to think.
"I want to see my family," she said.

The emperor gave Mulan the fastest horse in the country.
And she quickly got on the horse.
She went over mountains and crossed shallow rivers.
She also passed by the Yellow River.
And Mulan finally returned to her village.

Mulan's family was so happy to see her.

Her father smiled widely.

He wanted to hug his daughter quickly.

But his legs were even weaker now.

"My daughter, you have been brave and strong," said her father.

Mulan's adventure was over.

She took off the armor and wore her dress.

Her hair also grew longer again.

One day, Mulan's fellow soldiers came to her house.
They saw Mulan and were shocked.
They never imagined she was a woman.

Mulan's story was told for many years.
She taught people that anyone can be a hero.

◆ Mulan

Once / there was a **girl** / named Mu**lan**.

She **li**ved in a **small vil**lage / in **Chi**na.

She had a **kind fa**ther / and a **lo**ving **mo**ther.

She **al**so had a **play**ful / **young**er **bro**ther.

Mu**lan** / **lo**ved to **play** out**side**.

She could **climb trees** / and **run fast**.

She **laugh**ed a **lot** / every **day**.

Her **laugh** / made her **fa**mily **smi**le.

Mu**lan**'s **fa**ther and **mo**ther / were **wea**vers.

They made **beau**tiful **clo**thes.

Sometimes, / Mu**lan**'s **fa**ther **told** her / **great sto**ries.

They were about **war**riors / and **he**roes.

Mu**lan li**ked to **hear** / those **sto**ries.

She did **not want** / to be a **wea**ver.

She **want**ed to be a **he**ro / some**day**.

She **dream**ed of ad**ven**tures.

◆ 뮬란

옛날 옛날에, 뮬란이라는 이름의 소녀가 있었습니다.

뮬란은 중국의 작은 마을에 살았어요.

그녀에게는 자상한 아버지와 사랑 많은 어머니가 계셨어요.

그녀에게는 개구쟁이 남동생도 있었습니다.

뮬란은 밖에서 노는 것을 좋아했습니다.

그녀는 나무를 잘 탔고, 달리기가 빨랐어요.

그녀는 매일 많이 웃었습니다.

뮬란의 웃음은 가족을 미소 짓게 했어요.

뮬란의 아버지와 어머니는 베를 짜는 사람들이었습니다.

그들은 아름다운 옷감을 만들었어요.

가끔, 뮬란의 아버지는 그녀에게 웅장한 이야기들을 들려주었습니다.

전사들과 영웅들에 관한 이야기들이었어요.

뮬란은 그 이야기 듣는 것을 좋아했습니다.

그녀는 베 짜는 사람이 되고 싶지 않았어요.

그녀는 언젠가 영웅이 되고 싶었습니다.

뮬란은 모험을 꿈꿨어요.

One day, / Mulan's **family** / **got** a **let**ter.

It was from the **em**peror.

The **em**peror needed **sold**iers / to **fight** for the **coun**try.

The **sold**iers / **had** to go to **Black Moun**tain.

The **na**me of Mulan's **fa**ther / was on the **list**.

Mulan's **fa**ther / was **on**ce a **great sol**dier.

But **now**, / he was a **weak** old **man**.

Mulan **saw** / her **fa**ther's **wor**ried **face**.

"I am **weak**. / But I will **fight** / for my **coun**try," / said her **fa**ther.

But Mulan / **felt** a **big sad**ness / in her **heart**.

'If **fa**ther **go**es, / he may **die**.

My **bro**ther / is **too young** to **go**,' / she thought.

She could **not** let / her **fa**ther **go**.

That night, / Mulan **had** an i**dea**.

It was a **big** / and **bold** i**dea**.

She was **go**ing / to be a **sol**dier.

'I will **do** it / for my **fa**ther!' / she thought.

28

어느 날, 뮬란의 가족은 편지 한 통을 받았습니다.
황제로부터 온 편지였어요.
황제는 나라를 위해 싸울 병사들이 필요했어요.
병사들은 검은 산으로 가야 했습니다.
뮬란 아버지의 이름이 명단에 올라 있었습니다.
뮬란의 아버지는 한때 훌륭한 병사였습니다.
하지만 지금 그는 쇠약한 노인이었어요.

뮬란은 아버지의 걱정 가득한 얼굴을 보았습니다.
"나는 쇠약해. 하지만 나라를 위해 싸우련다." 그녀의 아버지가 말했습니다.
뮬란은 가슴 깊이 큰 슬픔을 느꼈어요.
'전쟁에 나가시면, 아버지는 돌아가실 거야.
남동생은 전쟁에 나가기에는 너무 어리고.' 그녀가 생각했습니다.
뮬란은 아버지가 전쟁에 나가도록 내버려둘 수 없었어요.

그날 밤, 뮬란은 좋은 생각이 떠올랐습니다.
크고 대담한 생각이었죠.
뮬란은 병사가 되기로 결심했어요.
'아버지를 위해 이 일을 해내겠어!' 그녀가 생각했습니다.

The **next** day, **/** Mu**lan** woke **up ear**ly.

She **act**ed on her i**dea**.

Mu**lan went** to the **mar**ket **/** in the **East**.

And she **bought /** a **big** and **strong hor**se.

Mu**lan al**so **went** to the **mar**ket **/** in the **West**.

And she **bought** a **sad**dle.

Mu**lan then / went** to the **mar**ket **/** in the **North**.

And she **bought /** a **big** and **hea**vy **ar**mor.

Finally, **/** Mu**lan went** to the **mar**ket **/** in the **South**.

She **bought /** a **sharp sword**.

Night came, **/** and Mu**lan ti**ed her **hair up**.

She **look**ed **/** like a **man**.

'I am **all rea**dy!' **/** Mu**lan** thought.

Mu**lan** did **not want /** to **wa**ke her **fa**mily.

She said good**bye** to them **/** in her **heart**.

Mu**lan / got** onto her **hor**se.

She **ro**de into the **night**.

It was **dark**, **/** so she **felt sca**red.

But she **want**ed to be **bra**ve.

She was **go**ing to be a **he**ro.

다음 날, 뮬란은 일찍 일어났습니다.
그녀는 자신의 생각을 행동으로 옮겼어요.
뮬란은 동쪽에 있는 시장에 갔습니다.
그리고 그녀는 크고 튼튼한 말을 샀어요.
뮬란은 서쪽에 있는 시장에도 갔습니다.
그리고 그녀는 안장을 샀어요.
그리고 나서 뮬란은 북쪽에 있는 시장에 갔습니다.
그리고 그녀는 크고 무거운 갑옷을 샀어요.
마지막으로, 뮬란은 남쪽에 있는 시장에 갔습니다.
그녀는 날카로운 검을 샀어요.

밤이 되었고, 뮬란은 머리를 올려 묶었습니다.
그녀는 남자처럼 보였어요.
'이제 준비가 다 되었어!' 뮬란이 생각했습니다.

뮬란은 가족을 깨우고 싶지 않았습니다.
그녀는 그들에게 마음속으로 작별 인사를 했어요.

뮬란은 자신의 말에 올라탔습니다.
그녀는 밤길을 달려 나갔습니다.
사방이 어두웠고, 뮬란은 무서웠어요.
하지만 그녀는 용감해지고 싶었습니다.
뮬란은 영웅이 되고자 했어요.

Mu**lan ro**de **/** for **ma**ny **hours**.

She **went** over **moun**tains **/** and **cross**ed **shal**low **ri**vers.

The **hor**se **/** was **ve**ry **fast**.

It **look**ed like **/** it was **fly**ing.

The **stars** shone **bright**ly **/** a**bo**ve Mu**lan**.

The **moon** **/** **led** her **way**.

Mu**lan** **/** **thought** about her **fa**mily.

She **miss**ed them al**rea**dy.

But she **knew** **/** she was **do**ing the **right** thing.

Mu**lan stop**ped **/** at the **Yel**low **Ri**ver.

She **slept** there **/** with her **hor**se.

In the **mor**ning, **/** Mu**lan** ar**ri**ved **/** at **Black Moun**tain.

She **saw ma**ny **sol**diers.

'They **look** very **strong**,' **/** Mu**lan** thought.

She **took** a **deep breath**.

She was **rea**dy **/** to **start** her **big** adven**ture**.

Mu**lan** trained **well /** with the **o**ther **sol**diers.

She was **strong**, **/** and she be**came strong**er.

No one **knew /** she was a **wo**man.

32

뮬란은 여러 시간 말을 타고 달렸습니다.
그녀는 산을 넘고 얕은 강을 건넜어요.
뮬란의 말은 매우 빨랐습니다.
마치 하늘을 나는 것만 같았어요.

별들이 뮬란의 머리 위에서 밝게 빛났습니다.
달이 그녀의 길을 안내했어요.
뮬란은 가족을 떠올렸습니다.
그녀는 벌써 가족이 보고 싶었습니다.
하지만 그녀는 자신이 옳은 일을 하고 있다는 것을 알았어요.

뮬란은 황허강에서 멈췄습니다.
그녀는 말과 함께 그곳에서 잠을 청했어요.
아침에, 뮬란은 검은 산에 도착했습니다.
그녀는 많은 병사들을 보았어요.
'저들은 아주 강해 보이는군.' 뮬란이 생각했습니다.
그녀는 숨을 깊게 들이쉬었어요.
뮬란은 큰 모험을 시작할 준비가 되었습니다.

뮬란은 다른 병사들과 함께 훈련했습니다.
그녀는 강했고, 더 강해졌어요.
아무도 뮬란이 여자인 줄 몰랐습니다.

Mulan also learned / to ride a horse / in a battle.
She loved riding / her strong and fast horse.
When she rode her horse, / she felt free.

Mulan also learned archery.
At first, / the arrows / missed the target.
But she kept trying.
Soon, / she was able to hit the target.
Other young soldiers / clapped for her.

Mulan soon made friends / in the camp.
They liked her / because she was strong / and kind.
The captain / always wanted Mulan / by his side.
He knew / she was a great soldier.

At night, / Mulan thought about her home.
She looked at the stars / and felt a little sad.
She missed her mother, / father, / and brother.
But she knew / she was doing something important.

Days / turned into weeks.
Mulan became / a brave and strong soldier.
She was ready / to fight in battles.

뮬란은 전쟁에서 말 타는 법도 배웠습니다.
뮬란은 튼튼하고 빠른 말 타는 것을 아주 좋아했어요.
그녀는 말을 탈 때마다 자유로운 기분이 들었습니다.

뮬란은 활 쏘는 법도 배웠습니다.
처음에는, 화살들이 과녁을 빗나갔어요.
하지만 뮬란은 계속해서 연습했습니다.
곧, 그녀는 과녁을 명중시킬 수 있었어요.
다른 젊은 병사들이 그녀에게 박수를 보냈습니다.

뮬란은 군영에서 금세 친구를 사귀었습니다.
뮬란이 강하고 친절했기 때문에 모두 그녀를 좋아했어요.
장군은 늘 뮬란을 곁에 두고 싶어 했지요.
장군은 뮬란이 훌륭한 병사라는 것을 알았어요.

밤이면, 뮬란은 집을 생각했습니다.
그녀는 별들을 바라보며 조금 울적해졌어요.
그녀는 어머니, 아버지, 그리고 남동생이 보고 싶었어요.
하지만 뮬란은 자신이 중요한 일을 하고 있다는 것을 알았습니다.

여러 날이 흘러 몇 주가 지났습니다.
뮬란은 용감하고 강한 병사가 되었어요.
그녀는 전쟁에서 싸울 준비가 되었습니다.

Then **one** day, **/** the **cap**tain had **big news**.

There was **go**ing to be a **bat**tle.

The **sol**diers **/ had** to **fight** the **e**nemy.

Mu**lan felt** a **lit**tle **sca**red **/** but **al**so **rea**dy.

She re**mem**bered her **train**ing.

The **sol**diers **/** put **on** their **ar**mors **/** and got **rea**dy.

They **took** their **swords /** and **bows**.

The **cap**tain **/ told** the **sol**diers **/** to be **strong** and **bra**ve.

Mu**lan lis**tened and **nod**ded.

She re**mem**bered her **fam**ily **/** and **felt bra**ver.

The **sol**diers **march**ed **/** to the **bat**tlefield.

Mu**lan saw** the **e**nemy **/** but she was **not** a**fraid**.

She was **rea**dy **/** to **fight** for her **coun**try.

The **bat**tle be**gan /** with **loud noi**ses.

The **sol**diers **ran /** as **fast** as they **could**.

Swords clashed, **/** and **ar**rows were **shot**.

Mu**lan fought /** with **all** her **heart**.

그러던 어느 날, 장군은 중요한 소식을 들었습니다.
전쟁이 벌어질 예정이었어요.
병사들은 적군과 싸워야 했습니다.
뮬란은 조금 두려웠지만, 동시에 모두 준비된 느낌도 들었어요.
그녀는 자신의 훈련을 떠올렸어요.

군인들은 갑옷을 입고 준비를 마쳤습니다.
그들은 검과 활을 챙겼어요.
장군은 병사들에게 강하고 용감해지라고 말했습니다.
뮬란은 장군의 말을 들으며 고개를 끄덕였어요.
가족을 떠올리자 더욱 용기가 났어요.

군인들은 전쟁터로 행군했습니다.
뮬란은 적군을 보았지만 두렵지 않았어요.
그녀는 나라를 위해 싸울 준비가 되어 있었어요.

커다란 소음과 함께 전쟁이 시작되었습니다.
병사들은 전력을 다해 달렸습니다.
검들이 부딪치는 소리가 났고, 화살들이 발사되었습니다.
뮬란은 온 힘을 다해 싸웠어요.

Mu**lan u**sed her **sword** / and her **bow**.
She was **fast**, / **strong**, / and **smart**.
She **help**ed her **cap**tain / **ma**ny times.
Her **cap**tain **al**so **help**ed **her** / **ma**ny times.

Then Mu**lan** / **saw** the **cap**tain / of the **e**nemy.
He was **try**ing / to **hurt** her **friends**.
He **mo**ved **fast**, / but Mu**lan** moved **fast**er.
She **u**sed her **bow** / and got **rid** of him.

The **e**nemy **saw** / Mu**lan**'s **bra**very and **strength**.
They were **sca**red / and ran a**way**.
Mu**lan help**ed her **coun**try / **win** the **bat**tle.
Everyone **cheer**ed / and **clap**ped.
They were **hap**py / and **proud**.

After the **bat**tle, / the **cap**tain **thank**ed Mu**lan**.
"You are the **bra**vest **sol**dier," / he said.
"You are my **good fri**end, too."
Mu**lan smil**ed, / **feel**ing **ve**ry **proud**.

38

뮬란은 그녀의 검과 활을 사용했습니다.
그녀는 빠르고, 강하고, 똑똑했어요.
뮬란은 여러 번 장군을 도왔습니다.
장군 또한 뮬란을 여러 번 도왔어요.

그때 뮬란은 적군의 대장을 보았습니다.
그는 뮬란의 친구들을 해치려 하고 있었어요.
그는 빠르게 움직였지만, 뮬란이 더 빨랐습니다.
그녀는 활을 사용해서 적군의 대장을 제거했어요.

적군은 뮬란의 용기와 힘을 보았습니다.
그들은 겁에 질려서 달아났어요.
뮬란은 자신의 나라가 전쟁에서 승리하도록 도왔습니다.
모두가 환호하고 박수를 쳤어요.
그들은 행복하고 자랑스러웠습니다.

전쟁이 끝나고, 장군이 뮬란에게 감사를 표했습니다.
"자네는 가장 용맹한 병사야." 그가 말했습니다.
"또한, 자네는 나의 좋은 친구야."
아주 뿌듯해하면서, 뮬란은 미소를 지었어요.

Mulan became famous / among all the soldiers.
The captain took her / to all the battles.
Mulan fought many battles / and won.
She was a soldier / for twelve years.
She was tired / but happy.

The captain told the emperor / about Mulan.
"He is a good soldier!
I want to see him," / said the emperor.
Then, / he invited Mulan / to the palace.

"I heard / you are a good soldier.
Ask me anything / you wish to have," / said the emperor.
Mulan did not / need to think.
"I want to see my family," / she said.

The emperor / gave Mulan the fastest horse / in the country.
And she quickly / got on the horse.
She went over mountains / and crossed shallow rivers.
She also / passed by the Yellow River.
And Mulan finally / returned to her village.

뮬란은 모든 병사들 사이에서 유명해졌습니다.
장군은 뮬란을 모든 전투에 데리고 다녔어요.
뮬란은 많은 전투에서 싸우고 승리했습니다.
그녀는 12년 동안 병사로 살았습니다.
뮬란은 피곤했지만 행복했어요.

장군은 황제에게 뮬란에 대해 이야기했습니다.
"그는 훌륭한 병사로군!
나는 그를 만나고 싶네." 황제가 말했습니다.
이윽고, 황제는 뮬란을 궁전으로 초대했어요.

"나는 자네가 훌륭한 병사라고 들었네.
자네가 갖고 싶은 것은 무엇이든 나에게 청해 보게." 황제가 말했습니다.
뮬란은 생각할 필요가 없었습니다.
"저는 제 가족을 만나고 싶습니다." 뮬란이 말했어요.

황제는 뮬란에게 나라에서 가장 빠른 말을 주었습니다.
그녀는 재빨리 말에 올라탔어요.
뮬란은 산을 넘고 얕은 강을 건넜습니다.
그녀는 황허강도 지났어요.
그리고 뮬란은 마침내 자신의 마을로 돌아왔습니다.

Mulan's **fa**mily **/** was **so hap**py to **see** her.

Her **fa**ther **smi**led **wi**dely.

He **want**ed to **hug** his **daugh**ter **/** **quick**ly.

But his **legs /** were even **weak**er **now**.

"My **daugh**ter, **/** you have been **bra**ve and **strong**," **/** said her **fa**ther.

Mulan's ad**ven**ture was **o**ver.

She took **off** the **ar**mor **/** and **wo**re her **dress**.

Her **hair /** **al**so **grew long**er a**gain**.

One day, **/** Mu**lan**'s **fe**llow **sol**diers **ca**me to her **hou**se.

They **saw** Mu**lan /** and were **shock**ed.

They **ne**ver i**ma**gined **/** she was a **wo**man.

Mulan's **sto**ry **/** was **told** for **ma**ny **years**.

She **taught peo**ple **/** that **any**one **/** can be a **he**ro.

뮬란의 가족은 그녀를 보고 매우 기뻐했습니다.
그녀의 아버지는 활짝 웃었어요.
그는 얼른 딸을 안고 싶었습니다.
하지만 그의 다리는 이전보다 더 쇠약했어요.
"내 딸아, 넌 정말 용감하고 강인했구나." 뮬란의 아버지가 말했습니다.

뮬란의 모험은 끝났습니다.
그녀는 갑옷을 벗고 자신의 옷을 입었어요.
머리도 다시 길렀습니다.

어느 날, 뮬란의 동료 병사들이 그녀의 집에 찾아왔습니다.
그들은 뮬란을 보고 충격을 받았습니다.
그들은 뮬란이 여자라고는 상상도 못했어요.

뮬란의 이야기는 오랫동안 전해졌습니다.
그녀는 누구나 영웅이 될 수 있다는 것을 일깨워 주었답니다.

Part 1 ◆ p.8~15

Mulan, hero, dream

letter, soldier, weak

idea, market, buy

night, horse, brave

archery, target, clap

battle, fight, use

emperor, invite, wish

family, brave, adventure

Summary

trained   hero   man   weak   emperor

Once upon a time, there was a girl named Mulan. She lived in a small village in China. When Mulan's father was called to war, he was too _____ and old to fight. So Mulan decided to go in his place. She dressed as a _____ and joined the army. She _____ hard and became a strong soldier. Mulan fought in many battles and helped her country win. After twelve years, the _____ praised her and let her return home. Mulan's story showed that anyone can be a _____ .

Memo

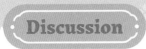
Discussion

1 ◆ (If you are a parent, please be prepared with your own response in case your child cannot think of an answer.) Mulan was scared but went to the army for her father. Have you ever done something you were afraid of for your parents?

(여러분이 부모라면, 아이가 대답을 생각하지 못할 수 있으니 여러분의 경험을 미리 생각해 두었다가 들려주세요.) 뮬란은 두려웠지만 나이 든 아버지를 위해 대신 군대에 갔어요. 여러분도 하기 싫고 두려웠지만, 사랑하는 엄마와 아빠를 위해 용기를 내서 했던 일이 있나요?

2 ◆ (If you are a parent, please be prepared with your own response in case your child cannot think of an answer.) Mulan could not shoot arrows well at first, but she kept practicing and became really good. Is there something you were not good at first, but got better at with practice? What was it? And how did you keep practicing even when it was hard?

(여러분이 부모라면, 아이가 대답을 생각하지 못할 수 있으니 여러분의 경험을 미리 생각해 두었다가 들려주세요.) 뮬란은 처음에 활을 잘 쏘지 못했지만, 계속 연습해서 결국 굉장히 잘하게 되었어요. 여러분도 처음에는 못했지만, 끊임없이 연습해서 잘하게 된 것이 있나요? 그것이 무엇인가요? 그리고 힘들었을 텐데 어떻게 포기하지 않고 계속 연습할 수 있었나요?

낭독하는 명작동화 Level 3-3
Mulan

초판 1쇄 발행 2024년 12월 2일

지은이 새벽달(남수진) 이현석 롱테일 교육 연구소
책임편집 강지희 | **편집** 명채린 백지연 홍하늘
디자인 박새롬 | **그림** 윤승일
마케팅 두잉글 사업본부

펴낸이 이수영
펴낸곳 롱테일북스
출판등록 제2015-000191호
주소 04033 서울특별시 마포구 양화로 113, 3층(서교동, 순흥빌딩)
전자메일 team@ltinc.net

이 도서는 대한민국에서 제작되었습니다.
롱테일북스는 롱테일㈜의 출판 브랜드입니다.

ISBN 979-11-93992-27-2 14740

Mulan

6

tie
man
ready

새벽달 X 이현석 낭독스쿨

Mulan

5

act on
market
buy

새벽달 X 이현석 낭독스쿨

Mulan

8

archery
target
clap

새벽달 X 이현석 낭독스쿨

Mulan

7

ride
brave
mountains

새벽달 X 이현석 낭독스쿨

Mulan

10

begin
run
fight

새벽달 X 이현석 낭독스쿨

Mulan

9

battle
enemy
remember

새벽달 X 이현석 낭독스쿨

Mulan

12

thank
bravest
famous

새벽달 X 이현석 낭독스쿨

Mulan

11

win
cheer
proud

새벽달 X 이현석 낭독스쿨